GOD
at work in our
DREAMS

Farai Mutsambiwa

DIAMOND MEDIA PRESS CO.
1-888-322-7392
https://www.diamondmediapressco.com/

ISBN Paperback: 978-1-951302-37-5

Contents

LETTER FROM FARAI...i

INTRODUCTION iii

1. WHY DO WE DREAM? 1

2. WHO IS THE SOURCE OF OUR DREAMS?.................................3

3. DREAMS OF GUIDANCE AND PROTECTION..........................5

4. DREAMS OF PROSPERITY 19

5. VISIONS OF HOPE AND CONFIRMATION 23

6. BAD DREAMS 29

7. SOME COMMON SYMBOLS...35

8.MISLEADING DREAMS 43

9.OTHER DREAMS IN THE BIBLE AND WHAT GOD CAN DO FOR YOU...49

10.HERE IS HOW IT WORKS 57

11.THE LORD IS MY SHEPHERD 63

12.CONCLUSION...69

ACKNOWLEDGEMENTS

This book is based on my personal experiences with dreams and my quest for answers, which I later found in the Holy Bible.

I want to say a special thank you to:

Rev. Tim and Vanessa Norman for kindly agreeing to edit and review this book for spiritual correctness.

My mother, Rev. Sophie Mutsambiwa, for teaching me the basics of dream interpretation when I was a young inquisitive boy.

My lovely wife, Jo, and children, and sister in law, Christine, who prayed for me and allowed me the space to write this book.

To my friend, Dave MacLellan, I thank you for being God-sent just at the right time to give the final push needed to make this miracle happen.

Last, but not least, my precious God, His Son, Jesus Christ, and the Holy Spirit, who inspired me, gave me the wisdom, cheered me on when I was feeling discouraged, and who impressed upon me that the time was now ripe for me to write my first book, a thing I have always wanted to do for a long time.

LETTER FROM FARAI

I don't know about you, but I have had many questions in life and have always wanted to hear the latest from my Maker, the King of the Universe.

If this is you, then I want to introduce you to what God has taught me about dreams. I believe that God wants you to find out for yourself the secret behind those dreams and visions when you are asleep. Like me, you will soon discover these are not mere visions but tones of supernatural intelligence.

I am happy that you are reading this book, as this is an answer to my prayer that through the wisdom God has given me on interpreting my own dreams, I may be able to bless many people all over the world, whether or not they believe in the LORD Jesus Christ.

Come along with me on this interesting life time journey. I am praying you will!

"Let the whole world sing to the Lord! Tell the good news every day about how he saves us. Tell all the nations how wonderful he is! Tell people everywhere about the amazing things he does,"1 Chronicles 16:23-24 (ERV).

INTRODUCTION

The bible teaches that God is the Source of all wisdom and that he created everything. Logic, therefore, tells me that if He created nature, he knows how it functions, and if I have a special occasion and would like good weather, I can ask him to intervene and turn a rainy day to a bright, sunny day.

I read about George Washington Carver, a famous American scientist who asked God about what he could do with a peanut, and God showed him how to make so many products from peanuts.
Similarly, if I had a question about future events that will affect my life and my nation, God should be able to tell me.

In this book, I explore the subject of dreams as one of the many ways God was able to communicate future events to people in the bible. As a little boy, I had many questions about my life and future. After searching many places for answers, and all in vain, I came across many amazing situations in the bible where God showed people what was going to happen and what to do.

I became so inspired that I craved this gift. Little did I know that God would answer that silent prayer. By searching the scriptures for related examples, I soon discovered that it is possible to observe one's dreams and to discern their meaning. This book, therefore, shares what God has taught me over many years. All bible quotations are either from the Easy-to-Read Bible Version (ERV), New Living Translation (NLT), or Amplified Bible Translation (AMP).

CHAPTER 1
WHY DO WE DREAM?

In the book of Amos, the bible notes in chapter 3 verse 7, "When the Lord God decides to do something, he will first tell his servants, the prophets." In this generation, and since more than 2,000 years ago when God gave the world a special gift of His Son, Jesus Christ, to secure and show us the way to salvation, every person that has accepted Jesus Christ as their LORD and Saviour is God's prophet here on earth.

1 Peter 2 vs 4-5, God says of us:

The Lord Jesus is the living stone. The people of the world decided that they did not want this stone. But he is the one God chose as one of great value. So, come to him. You also are like living stones, and God is using you to build a spiritual house. You are to serve God in this house as holy priests, offering him spiritual sacrifices that he will accept because of Jesus Christ.

As his holy priests or prophets, God would like all believers to be the first people to know what he is going to do in our family, village, town, church, country, and even the world. And with the way things are going in our generation, I don't know about you, but I would like to be warned about where and how to invest my money, when and how to travel from point A to B, and so on.

In Genesis Chapter 18 is a fascinating story of how God was planning to visit Sodom and Gomorrah to see for himself and confirm, first hand, the rumours He had heard of the wickedness of these two cities. I like what God said in verses 17 – 19:

Should I hide my plan from Abraham? the LORD *asked. "For Abraham will certainly become a great and mighty nation, and all the nations of the earth will be blessed through him. I have singled him out so that he will direct his sons and their families to keep the way of the* LORD *by doing what is right and just. Then I will do for Abraham all that I have promised."*

So the LORD *told Abraham, "I have heard a great outcry from Sodom and Gomorrah, because their sin is so flagrant. I am going down to see if their actions are as wicked as I have heard. If not, I want to know."*

How would you feel if God were to visit your town or city and say, "Hmmm, I am about to do such and such a thing, but I just can't do it without first telling Dave, Sam, and Flo!"

Again, I don't know about you, but this is what I always wanted to happen when I was little boy. I still desire to be so close to my precious LORD that, like father Abraham, I want God to say, "I cannot hide my plans from my son, Farai."

CHAPTER 2
WHO IS THE SOURCE OF OUR DREAMS?

The bible is replete with many incidents, skirmishes, and battles between God's chosen people, Israel, and people of other nations, e.g. the Amalekites, Ammonites, Philistines, etc.

One of my favourite encounters is recorded in 2 Kings Chapter 6 vs 8 to 12:

> *When the king of Aram was at war with Israel, he would confer with his officers and say, "We will mobilize our forces at such and such a place."*
>
> *But immediately Elisha, the man of God, would warn the king of Israel, "Do not go near that place, for the Arameans are planning to mobilize their troops there." So the king of Israel would send word to the place indicated by the man of God. Time and again, Elisha warned the king, so that he would be on the alert there.*
>
> *The king of Aram became very upset over this. He called his officers together and demanded, "Which of you is the traitor? Who has been informing the king of Israel of my plans?"*
>
> *"It's not us, my lord the king," one of the officers replied. "Elisha, the prophet in Israel, tells the king of Israel even the words you speak in the privacy of your bedroom!"*

What an anointed man of God! As I have said before, we are living in a dangerous world in which no one seems to have a solution. What do we do in such times as these?

Only Jesus Christ and our relationship with Him is the answer.

Here is what the bible admonishes in 1 John 5 vs 1 – 5:

By our faith in Jesus Christ, we do good works, and we believe in a miracle-working God who multiplies two fishes and five loaves of bread to feed more than five thousand people, who raises people from the dead, who can command tornadoes to fall apart, who can heal people of cancers, who can stop the entire universe to prove to one man that he will be healed in three days' time, who can turn water into wine, the One who walks on water, and of course, the God who can warn us about what is going to happen tomorrow or ten years from now through visions.

That is the God I worship and am talking about. The Prince of Peace, the Great Physician, the Provider and the Source, the Ever-Present Help in times of need, the God who is everywhere at the same time, the Rock of Escape, and many other names. Now come and explore with me how He can tell you about the future in a dream.

CHAPTER 3
DREAMS OF GUIDANCE AND PROTECTION

As I have read the Bible, I find that it sheds light on the meanings of many different visions and symbols. As I write this book, one of my prayers is: "Lord, how can a simple man possibly know and, furthermore, interpret the vast permutations of dreams all people could possibly have?" Because of this, I cannot, therefore, claim I know everything or how to interpret every possible dream. Rather, my assignment is to give a possible guideline, based on the word of the Living God and my personal experience, rather than a psycho-analytical assessment of dreams. My hope is that this outline will set you off on an interesting journey of asking God, the King of the Universe, to give you the Spirit of discernment of visions not only for the good of yourself, your family, and community but also the entire world.

In all this, rest assured, He will answer your prayer as this is already His desire and will as confirmed by the scriptures:

Joel chapter 2 vs 28 – 29:

"Then, after doing all those things, I will pour out my Spirit upon all people. Your sons and daughters will prophesy. Your old men will dream dreams, and your young men will see visions. In those days I will pour out my Spirit even on servants—men and women alike."

And again in Acts 2 vs 17 – 18, when the apostles were commissioned by the Holy Spirit to do their job of preaching the gospel to all nations and therefore, start the first church:

'In the last days,' God says, 'I will pour out my Spirit upon all people. Your sons and daughters will prophesy. Your young men will see visions, and your old men will dream dreams. In those days I will pour out my Spirit even on my servants—men and women alike— and they will prophesy.'

THE DISCIPLES RECEIVE
GUIDANCE THROUGH A DREAM

All bible readers will be familiar with the fact that, after Jesus was crucified and rose from the dead on the 3rd day, He spent the next 40 days on earth meeting His disciples and many other chosen people. After this, He ascended into heaven before the very eyes of His disciples, leaving them a commandment to *"Go into all the world and preach the Good News to everyone…"* (Mark 16:15)

After waiting for and receiving the Holy Spirit as Jesus had also instructed, the disciples went about preaching the Good News about the coming of Jesus and what He had done for humanity on the cross, beginning in Jerusalem, throughout Judea, and then in Samaria. The disciples shared this Good News only with Jewish people and seemed to be reluctant to go beyond and share the same with non-Jewish people or gentiles in Israel and other nations as Jesus had commanded them to do until God intervened.

This is how it happened. There was a non-Jewish Roman officer by the name Cornelius who lived in Caesarea city, Israel. He was God fearing and always prayed and gave to the poor. One day as he was praying, God sent him an Angel to tell him to send his servants to a nearby city called Joppa to invite Simon Peter to come and share the Good News with him and his family.

At the place he was staying, Simon Peter was very hungry and fell into a trance as he waited for lunch to be prepared and served. He then had a dream or vision in which God was asking him to eat some food, which, according to Jewish culture, was untouchable. In the dream, God said to him, "Do not call something unclean if God has made it clean." This dream or vision was repeated three times.

As Simon Peter was pondering what this all meant, the servants sent by Cornelius arrived and delivered their message for him to come and preach the Good News to the Roman Officer. The Holy Spirit also confirmed to Simon Peter that it was indeed God that had sent for him to go to Caesarea city and that this was the meaning of the dream in which he was being commanded to eat food Jewish tradition condemned as unclean. Since non-Jewish people were considered uncircumcised and unclean gentiles with no covenant with God, the Jews had nothing to do with them, and that explains why the disciples were unwilling to preach the Good News gospel to non-Jewish people as commanded by Jesus. When Simon Peter obeyed and preached the gospel of Jesus Christ to Cornelius and family, God confirmed His will to Peter and the rest of the disciples by allowing these gentiles to also receive the gift of the Holy Spirit just as the disciples had done.

In this dream or vision example from the bible, God is teaching us that He is always doing a new thing in our lives. That is, things we might have never experienced or heard of before. So, in order to give people the confidence to take up new challenges never done by any member of their family or something completely new and unique in human history, God can communicate this to them in a dream, following the pattern described in Peter's dream above. Notice how God used Peter's hunger to trigger a dream about food. This explains the notion that, when trying to interpret dreams, one must think about their immediate circumstances and what their goals and desires in life are.

Simon Peter and the other disciples had a mission to preach the gospel to the entire world, and at the time, they were not too sure that what Jesus had told them to do was really acceptable given the Jewish culture and tradition. He finally connected the dots when he had a unique dream, which was repeated three times, leaving him puzzled in search for an answer, and the coincidence of servants arriving just in time with an invitation to come to Caesarea city and do something not culturally acceptable. He knew then what God wanted him to do.

Again, you may be harbouring some dreams, goals, aspirations, or ambitions to do something, but then you may not be sure if this is what God wants you to do in life. You will obviously be praying for God to confirm the way. In this respect, watch out for dreams— good or strange— and try to relate them back to what you have been "hungry" for in life.

You will be amazed at how that will relate.

Man eating strange food

ANGELS

Although I have never dreamt of seeing angels, the Bible links angels with God's presence, guidance, favour, provision, protection, deliverance, and many other forms of supernatural occurrences. In Genesis 28, God gives us a glimpse of what seeing a vision of angels might mean in our lives.

"Jacob dreams of angels ascending a ladder to heaven"
from an engraving by Gustave Dore (1832 – 1883)

JACOB'S DREAM AT BETHEL
(GENESIS 28 VS 10 – 16: NLT BIBLE)

Meanwhile, Jacob left Beersheba and travelled toward Haran. At sundown he arrived at a good place to set up camp and stopped there for the night. Jacob found a stone to rest his head against and lay down to sleep. As he slept, he dreamed of a stairway that reached from the earth up to heaven. And he saw the angels of God going up and down the stairway.

At the top of the stairway stood the LORD, and he said, "I am the LORD, the God of your grandfather Abraham, and the God of your father, Isaac. The ground you are lying on belongs to you. I am giving it to you and your descendants. Your descendants will be as numerous as the dust of the earth! They will spread out in all directions—to the west and the east, to the north and the south. And all the families of the earth will be blessed through you and your descendants. What's more, I am with you, and I will protect you wherever you go. One day I will bring you back to this land. I will not leave you until I have finished giving you everything I have promised you."

Then Jacob awoke from his sleep and said, "Surely the LORD is in this place, and I wasn't even aware of it!"

Interpretation

After Jacob had fallen out with his brother, Esau, over a blessing, Jacob had to flee for his life to Haran. He must have been really concerned about his future. In this state of desperation, God showed Jacob a dream of what he was to become. It confirmed the blessing his father, Isaac, had conferred upon him earlier. The dream served to strengthen him for the years he was to be away from his family. Over time, God honoured what he had shown Jacob. If you read the story of Jacob in the bible, you will find that angels did help him reach his destiny in life. Today, the entire world is being blessed by Jesus Christ a descendant of Jacob showing that, God is always true to His word.

Take note of what Jacob said as soon as he woke up: "Surely the LORD is in this place, and I wasn't even aware of it!" If you care enough to remember your dreams and pray about them, God has a way of letting you know of His presence and the meaning of dreams He gives you.

DIRECT VISIONS

In many cases, God has given me direct visions of the things affecting my life. For example, I have had many dreams of family members being in trouble. As the Lord has taught me through the lives of the patriarchs like Abraham, who was in the habit of "falling face down on the ground" (Genesis 17 vs 1-2) at the appearance of God, I have always responded with reverence rather than brushing off such dreams with skepticism. I usually get out of bed and start to pray, and to my surprise, when I call the concerned relatives, even after a long time, they always tell me how God miraculously saved them from an experience I would have seen in a dream!

I am sure every believer in Christ will agree with God's word in James 5 vs 16 – 18, which instructs:

> *The earnest prayer of a righteous person has great power and produces wonderful results. Elijah was as human as we are, and yet when he prayed earnestly that no rain would fall, none fell for three and a half years! Then, when he prayed again, the sky sent down rain and the earth began to yield its crops.*

So, combining prayer with the visions shown will produce wonders.

MIST AND BRIGHT CLOUDS

In the bible, mist and bright clouds are often associated with the presence and glory of the Lord.

One example is when Jesus Christ went up a mountain with his disciples and was then transfigured and confirmed by God before them.
The bible (Matthew 17 vs 1 – 9) gives the following account:

> *"Six days later, Jesus took Peter, James, and John the brother of James and went up on a high mountain. They were all alone there. While these followers watched him, Jesus was changed. His face became bright like the sun, and his clothes became white as light. Then two men were there,*

talking with him. They were Moses and Elijah. Peter said to Jesus, "Lord, it is good that we are here. If you want, I will put three tents here—one for you, one for Moses, and one for Elijah." While Peter was talking, a bright cloud came over them. A voice came from the cloud and said, "This is my Son, the one I love. I am very pleased with him. Obey him!" The followers with Jesus heard this voice. They were very afraid, so they fell to the ground. But Jesus came to them and touched them. He said, "Stand up. Don't be afraid." The followers looked up, and they saw that Jesus was now alone. As Jesus and the followers were coming down the mountain, he gave them this command: "Don't tell anyone about what you saw on the mountain. Wait until the Son of Man has been raised from death. Then you can tell people about what you saw."

Interpretation

In 2001, I had a life changing experience with God. I had been honouring God through the payment of tithes and offerings to my church as specified in Malachi chapter 3 vs 10 in which God challenges all people to bring the full ten percent of their income and offerings to meet the church's expenses and in return, He promised to bless them beyond expectation.

I had been doing this for nearly five years, and nothing seemed to be happening. Then one night, I woke up angry and concerned, and I went into my living room to pray. I was living a miserable life of not having enough. I cried, questioning God why He was not responding to my prayers as promised to those that obey His commandments.

When I went to bed after the prayer, I thought I would die for the hard questions I had asked God. But to my utter surprise, He gave me a memorable vision of a massive white pillar of cloud or mist rising up from the earth into the skies.

I somehow knew beyond any shadow of doubt that my prayer had been answered. I went to sleep again, and God showed me another vision of me and my family bidding farewell to my parents. Within the next two weeks, I was offered a job in England. I had been living in Africa, and I desperately needed a more fulfilling job, and my expectation was I would find a local job. God graciously made me an heir to His written Will or promises in the bible.

For, *"if you belong to Christ, then you are Abraham's seed, and heirs according to the promise."* (Galatians 3 vs 29)

The Lord paid for my British Airways flight for interview, two more flights for me, and for my wife and children to come and settle in England. I was given free hotel accommodation for three weeks whilst seeking my own accommodation. My family joined me soon after a house was secured for us. To appreciate more how blessed we were, just imagine us moving to England from a third world country known for hyperinflation, shortage of almost everything, including basic food items in shops, and long queues to fill up the gas tank and access money in the bank.

To be honest, the move was beyond our wildest expectation, just as God promised in His word. Through this experience, I also learnt that God responds to passionate and frank prayer based on what He says He will do in the Bible.

The fact that God gave me a vision with the same meaning in two forms showed me that the answer was absolute as Joseph's dream recorded in the bible.

A pillar of white mist or cloud ascending into the sky

DREAMS OF AN OCEAN

Recently, my wife and I were praying to God many prayers concerning a difficult situation. We had found a bible scripture on the basis of which, we were petitioning God, but our prayers seemed to go unanswered, and for a very long time, there was no sign of change. Then one day, God gave my wife a scary dream.

She was walking with others along a bridge that was spanning across a converge place of two oceans. The waters in the oceans were not only enormous, but gigantic waves were threatening to sweep over her and other people on the bridge.

Bridge over ocean

Interpretation

When we prayed over the dream and its meaning, we discovered that it was a veiled, good warning from Almighty God to stop us doubting anything He has ever promised in the bible.

God gave us two scriptures to confirm what He was saying.
The first was 1 Corinthians 2: 9, which says:

"That is what the Scriptures mean when they say, 'No eye has seen, no ear has heard, and no mind has imagined what God has prepared for those who love him."

The second was a scripture taken from a situation recorded in 2 Kings 7. The bible says there was a famine in the city of Samaria in Israel because of enemy troops that besieged it. Then, one day, Elisha the Prophet prophesied that "by this time tomorrow in the markets of Samaria, six quarts of choice flour will cost only one piece of silver, and twelve quarts of barley grain will cost only one piece of silver." When the king's bodyguard heard this, he said to Elisha that "that couldn't happen even if the Lord opened the windows of heaven!" But Elisha replied, "You will see it happen with your own eyes, but you won't be able to eat any of it!"

Long story short, God performed a miracle. A lot of food was hastily abandoned by enemy troops outside the city when they mistakenly heard the sound of a mighty army approaching, concluding the king of Israel had secretly hired troops from other nations to come and help him. When this news was reported to people inside the besieged city of Samaria, they all rushed out of the city gate to gather the food. On that day, six quarts of choice flour was sold for one piece of silver, and twelve quarts of barley cost only one piece of silver on Samaria's markets. The king's bodyguard, who had doubted God, was stumbled to death by the rushing crowd as he was guarding the city gate.

Here is a great promise to anchor your hopes on, from Numbers 23 vs 19:

"God is not a man; he will not lie. God is not a human being; his decisions will not change. If he says he will do something, then he will do it. If he makes a promise, then he will do what he promised".

CHAPTER 4
DREAMS OF PROSPERITY

The foundational scripture is found in the story of Joseph, one of the many sons of Jacob, who was given two visions to show that one day, he would become a "Prime Minister" in Egypt (Genesis 37). One morning, whilst serving a jail sentence in that country, Joseph accurately interpreted the meaning of dreams of his two jail mates (Genesis 40). In Genesis 41, Joseph again accurately predicted the meaning of Pharaoh's dreams given in two forms. It was God's gift of wisdom to interpret dreams that suddenly made a way for Joseph to be released from jail to become Egypt's "Prime Minister."

PHARAOH'S DREAM
(GENESIS 41 VS 14 – 36)

So Pharaoh called Joseph from the prison. The guards quickly got Joseph out of prison. Joseph shaved, put on some clean clothes, and went to see Pharaoh. Pharaoh said to Joseph, "I had a dream, and no one can explain it for me. I heard that you can explain dreams when someone tells you about them."
Joseph answered, "I cannot! But God can explain the dream for you, Pharaoh."

Then Pharaoh said to Joseph, "In my dream I was standing by the Nile River. Seven cows came up out of the river and stood there eating the grass. They were healthy, good-looking cows. Then I saw seven more cows come up out of the river after them, but these cows were thin and looked sick. They were the worst cows I had ever seen anywhere in Egypt! The thin, sick cows ate the first healthy cows, but they still looked thin and sick. You couldn't even tell they had eaten the healthy cows. They looked as thin and sick as they did in the beginning. Then I woke up.

"In my next dream I saw seven heads of grain growing on one plant. They

were healthy and full of grain. And then seven more heads of grain grew after them, but they were thin and scorched by the hot wind. Then the thin heads of grain ate the seven good heads of grain.

"I told these dreams to my magicians. But no one could explain the dreams to me. What do they mean?"

Then Joseph said to Pharaoh, "Both of these dreams have the same meaning. God is telling you what will happen soon.
The seven good cows and the seven good heads of grain are seven good years. And the seven thin, sick-looking cows and the seven thin heads of grain mean that there will be seven years of hunger in this area. These seven bad years will come after the seven good years. God has shown you what will happen soon. He will make these things happen just as I told you. For seven years there will be plenty of food in Egypt. But then there will be seven years of hunger. The people will forget how much food there had been in Egypt before. This famine will ruin the country. It will be so bad that people will forget what it was like to have plenty of food.

"Pharaoh, you had two dreams about the same thing. That means God wanted to show you that he really will make this happen, and he will make it happen soon! So, Pharaoh, you should choose a wise, intelligent man and put him in charge of Egypt. Then you should choose other men to collect food from the people. During the seven good years, the people must give them one-fifth of all the food they grow. In this way these men will collect all the food during the seven good years and store it in the cities until it is needed. Pharaoh, this food will be under your control. Then during the seven years of hunger, there will be food for the country of Egypt. And Egypt will not be destroyed by the famine."

Interpretation

This experience tells me that it is God, and God alone, who gives people dreams and helps them interpret them. We are not given dreams in order to scare us but to give us warnings about the good and bad things to come.

As I will explain elsewhere in this book, when we see bad visions, we need to pray first for interpretation of the meaning. Once we know the meaning, we can either pray for God's protection or for Him to stop Satan's plans or His judgement if the vision is bad. Where a good vision is given, pray that He grants us the desires of our heart.

In this case, good dreams showing seven fat cows and seven full beautiful grain heads meant seven years of prosperity. Because the dreams were in two forms, it meant that it was too late and that God's plan was already established and set in motion. Joseph also sets us a good example that, when blessed by God with wisdom or anything else, we should be quick to give Him credit and never attribute His kindness to good luck, chance, or our own wisdom.

GAME

African Antelope

In 2000, when I was faced with a difficult decision whether or not to enroll on a Master's Degree, God showed me a vision of an antelope which I was trying to kill, but each time I tried to shoot it, I missed. I had enrolled for the Master's programme and did not have the money nor the courage to embark on the studies because the course outline showed the degree programme included a module on Decision Analysis involving statistics. Because I was weak at this subject, I felt overwhelmed and quickly quit the programme out of fear. Soon after that, I prayed to God and asked if I had made the right decision. That night, God showed me a vision of the antelope.

Interpretation

In their natural habitat, antelope and any other game are very elusive and not easy to find. So, I interpreted this to mean that God had given me an uncommon favour and opportunity to prosper, and if I missed this chance, there might never be another one. This secured my confidence to change my decision, and I went back to enroll on the Master's programme again. As if to confirm my interpretation, the course was already fully subscribed by the next day! Fortunately, I was informed, there was only one other person who had paid his fees but wanted to confirm his enrolment by the following Monday, and this was Friday.

Through prayer and by God's grace, the following Monday, the other person confirmed that he was quitting the programme. Phew! I got myself enrolled.

The rest is a story of how God intervened and paid the fees for me. I later approached Him in prayer for a good job, making reference to my Master's Degree that was now in hand and His faithfulness to make good every promise He has given in the bible, including the one on tithing, and that's when He gave me the vision I described earlier, of a white pillar of rising mist.

CHAPTER 5
VISIONS OF HOPE AND CONFIRMATION

RAIN

I have experienced many dreams of heavy showers of rain on me, particularly after works of righteousness, like giving to the poor. On one occasion, I was preparing for a journey to Brussels and was not confident about getting around to the meeting venue and whether I would secure enough appointments with the European Commission staff to make my visit worthwhile. I was also getting anxious about travel. After praying to God, I didn't get an answer for nearly two weeks. Instead, it came on the very last night before departure. This came in the form of a vision of heavy rainfall on me.

Interpretation

Not only did I have a very safe flight to Brussels and back home, I did not have trouble getting to the venue and had many appointments to meet all the people I wanted to see the moment I got there. My company benefitted immensely from my visit.

As you can already discern, rain dreams mean blessings and answered prayers. In the bible, God has always linked rain with His blessings. Deuteronomy chapter 11 vs 13 – 15 says,

"If you carefully obey all the commands I am giving you today, and if you love the LORD your God and serve him with all your heart and soul, then he will send the rains in their proper seasons—the early and late rains—so you can bring in your harvests of grain, new wine, and olive oil. He will give you lush pastureland for your livestock, and you yourselves will have all you want to eat."

Rain dreams have always confirmed and given me hope that what I have done is acceptable to God or that my plans will go on well, and they always have gone well!

Similarly, the night before the day I received good news from the original publishers of this book that I was to be awarded a contract, I had this dream: I was walking in a desert, and a huge rain cloud appeared. It was hanging right over me.

I have learnt that during periods of drought, farmers do what is called cloud seeding. I felt that since this was a cloud I had no control over, it was bound to float away or dissipate without dropping the rain if I did not pray. I prayed, asking God to bless me, and guess what? The next day, I received the good news.

Rainfall

RAINBOW

Similar to rain dreams, visions of rainbows in a dream have always confirmed that something good is about to happen and that whatever I am desiring and praying for at the time will indeed come to pass. A rainbow in the bible is associated with God's covenant relationship with His people.

For example, here is what God says in Genesis 9 vs 8 – 15 after all people of Noah's generation were killed by floods, except him and his family:

Then God told Noah and his sons, "I hereby confirm my covenant with you and your descendants, and with all the animals that were on the boat with you—the birds, the livestock, and all the wild animals—every living creature on earth. Yes, I am confirming my covenant with you. Never again will floodwaters kill all living creatures; never again will a flood destroy the earth."

 Then God said, "I am giving you a sign of my covenant with you and with all living creatures, for all generations to come. I have placed my rainbow in the clouds. It is the sign of my covenant with you and with all the earth. When I send clouds over the earth, the rainbow will appear in the clouds, and I will remember my covenant with you and with all living creatures. Never again will the floodwaters destroy all life. When I see the rainbow in the clouds, I will remember the eternal covenant between God and every living creature on earth." Then God said to Noah, "Yes, this rainbow is the sign of the covenant I am confirming with all the creatures on earth."

Rainbow

When my brother's 12-year-old son, who had learning difficulties, disappeared from home and boarded a coach to another town more than 600km away, we all prayed. We were desperate. After much prayer, that night, I saw a vision of a rainbow. The following morning, we heard the miracle news we all wanted to hear. He was safe. The boy had passed through a busy city, where he changed coaches and proceeded to his destination— without money! It also happened between sunset and midday the following day. Isn't our God awesome?

SUN, MOON AND STARS – DREAM OF ENCOURAGEMENT

Unlike the part of Europe where I now live, in Africa, we have long seasons of blazing sunshine. Maybe as a result of nostalgia, I have often had dreams in which I am walking or basking in bright sunshine. I have also had vivid dreams in which I have seen a beautiful constellation of stars and, sometimes, a gorgeous moon.

Beautiful moon

Interpretation

Genesis chapter 1 is an account of how God created the world. In verses 14 – 18, the Bible says God created the sun, moon, and stars and put them in the sky to rule over the day and over the night. They were also created as signs to mark the beginning and end of seasons, days, and years.
In Psalm 19, the bible says everything we see in the heavens shows God's glory, and in verse 3, it says, *"They speak without a sound or word; their voice is never heard."*

What are the heavens speaking of? When I see an amazingly beautiful house, common sense tells me that there must be a great architect who designed it. You can also think of any of your favourite car or brand, and you will see that behind it is a manufacturer. Your car or brand will usually come with a user-friendly manual as well! The heavens— including the sun, moon, and stars— are shouting day and night and throughout the whole world that there is a God in heaven – Creator of all things we see. This same God has also inspired some of the people we read about in the bible to write the Bible, a user-friendly manual to teach people how to live a successful life on earth. 2,000 years ago, God sent His own Son Jesus Christ in the form of a baby that grew like all of us do and became a man. He was so full of wisdom and taught people about heaven and many other things. Listen to one of His teachings in Matthew chapter 5 verse 15:

"...No one lights a lamp and then puts it under a basket. Instead, a lamp
is placed on a stand, where it gives light to everyone in the house..."

Friend, here is what dreams of the sun, moon and stars mean. God created each one of us and put us here on earth. He also hid many dreams or aspirations, gifts, and talents in us. These dreams and goals are unique, and often times, we spend our entire life trying to discover, develop, and implement them. Amazingly, the majority of us have allowed fear to hold us back.

So, when you consistently have dreams of the heavenly lights, God could be encouraging you, saying, "Hey, I have created you in My own image and have given you many dreams, gifts, and talents. . I did not mean for you to hide or bury them. You have been going round and round in the same place for a long time. It's now time for you to stir up your faith and start doing something about the plan and purpose I created you for. Rise up and shine in the world, like a light placed on a stand or a city built on a hill!"

Amongst other things, the sun is a symbol of God's everlasting power, presence, and protection. (Read Psalm 84:11). The moon speaks of His faithfulness (Read Psalms 89: 36 – 37), and stars show that, when God answers prayers, it will be beyond our greatest imagination. (Read Genesis 15: 1- 4)

CHAPTER 6
BAD DREAMS

Before I knew that God was always communicating with me through dreams, warning of impending dangers, I used to have some bad dreams which I ignored, and then, things would happen without me noticing, when, in fact, I had been previously warned in dreams.

Then one day, the Lord got my attention. I dreamt that I and my relatives were digging and building an earth mound.

When I woke up, I thought that this was just one of those bad dreams and went back to sleep. Then, the following morning, I was shattered to learn that my aunt and her husband had been involved in a fatal car accident and that the husband had died on the spot. When I was told the time the accident occurred, it was the same time I had had that dream.

As I was searching my soul for what this all meant, God led me to the following scriptures in the book of Amos chapter 7:

A VISION OF LOCUSTS

The Sovereign LORD showed me a vision. I saw him preparing to send a vast swarm of locusts over the land. This was after the king's share had been harvested from the fields and as the main crop was coming up. In my vision the locusts ate every green plant in sight. Then I said, "O Sovereign LORD, please forgive us or we will not survive, for Israel is so small."

So the LORD relented from this plan. "I will not do it," he said.

A VISION OF FIRE

Wild Fire

Then the Sovereign LORD showed me another vision. I saw him preparing to punish his people with a great fire. The fire had burned up the depths of the sea and was devouring the entire land.

Then I said, "O Sovereign LORD, please stop or we will not survive, for Israel is so small."

Then the LORD relented from this plan, too. "I will not do that either," said the Sovereign LORD.

A VISION OF A PLUMB LINE

A plumb line

Then he showed me another vision. I saw the Lord standing beside a wall that had been built using a plumb line. He was using a plumb line to see if it was still straight. And the LORD said to me, "Amos, what do you see?"

I answered, "A plumb line."

And the Lord replied, "I will test my people with this plumb line. I will no longer ignore all their sins. The pagan shrines of your ancestors will be ruined, and the temples of Israel will be destroyed; I will bring the dynasty of King Jeroboam to a sudden end."

Interpretation

There are two lessons that I drew out of these visions. Firstly, all three visions depicted something bad, and the bible makes it very clear that these were different forms of judgement that God wanted to inflict.
Secondly, God showed me that each time the prophet had prayed, God relented from executing the warning.
From the time I received this revelation, each time I saw bad pictures in my dream, I have learnt to treat this as a great favour from God, to warn me of something that would endanger my personal life, my family, or even my nation.

A few personal experiences will drive this fact home.

ATTACK BY A MADMAN

I have learnt from experience that this is one of the most serious warnings of personal harm one could possibly have.
I first learnt this from my mother, who always related a particular personal harmful incident to previous visions of an attack or curse by a madman in a dream.
Out of the few dreams I have had involving a madman, I will pick this example of what happened two days before Christmas day in 2009.

On 23rd December 2009, I had a very bad fall in the car park at home. The inclined pavement was covered with ice because of the bitterly cold weather. Both I and my two little children who witnessed the incident could not believe that despite the great fall, I got up without a broken bone or dislodged teeth. I personally attribute this to God's mercy.
As I went about my business after the accident, I couldn't help but thank God for giving me a good warning the previous night when I dreamt of being attacked by a madman. Because I knew what seeing a madman in a dream meant, I immediately woke up and prayed, pleading the blood of Jesus on all members of my household.
If I had not done so, I am fully convinced I would have ended up in hospital with a broken bone. As if to confirm my observation, when I told

my wife what had happened to me, she said I should really thank God for His protection. She mentioned that the Unit she works in at hospital had twelve admissions of people with broken bones that day, and out of these, five had broken limbs due to ice-induced falls. So, this wasn't mere luck; God had responded to my prayer, which I made immediately after the bad vision I had seen.

CHAPTER 7
SOME COMMON SYMBOLS

God uses everyday language and symbols to communicate messages in dreams, and the key to knowing what He is saying is to ask Him in prayer. In Proverbs chapter 25 vs 2, the bible teaches that:

It is God's privilege to conceal things, and the king's privilege
to discover them.

This simply means that if we want to be great or wise and powerful, we have to search for the hidden meaning of all things which happen to have been deliberately hidden by the Most-High God, Source of all wisdom.
Since my environment, culture, and upbringing will be different from that of every reader of this book, God will give each person symbols that may be similar or different from my own experiences.

Below, I give specific examples God gave me in various seasons of my life. He has always given me proof or enough evidence that, had I not prayed, I would have been the victim. For example, after asking God for protection, I have often observed that the bad things I dreamt about happened to other people or another nation instead of me or my nation, according to the word of God in Isaiah 43 vs 3 – 4, which says:

For I am the LORD, your God, the Holy One of Israel,
your Savior. I gave Egypt as a ransom for your freedom;
I gave Ethiopia and Seba in your place. Others were given
in exchange for you. I traded their lives for yours because
you are precious to me. You are honored, and I love you.

LIST OF COMMON SYMBOLS
AND WHAT THEY HAVE MEANT TO ME IN
MY EXPERIENCE

Ripe Fruit

- Bees – these have always been a warning of something deadly. To be precise, *beware of death*. *"O death, where is your sting?"* – 1 Corinthians 15 vs 55 says.

- Bread – pray as this may be danger. I will explain in the next chapter.

- Chewing gum – I will explain this a little more as it has both earthly and eternal consequences. Like most Christians do, I have, on many occasions, prayed, "Lord forgive my sins. Forgive the evil words I have spoken."

36

The result has been a dream in which I struggle pulling sticky chewing gum from my mouth and teeth after chewing it. This only confirms the power and earthly and eternal penalty of the idle words we speak, including condemning others. The bible severely warns in Romans 14 vs 12 – 13, *"Yes, each of us will give a personal account to God. So, let's stop condemning each other. Decide instead to live in such a way that you will not cause another believer to stumble and fall."*

•   Crops – green plants and crops often signify good health and good outcome.

•   Disaster – any visions of any form of disaster, pray that the devil's plans do not happen. I once dreamt of a fatal train accident. The following morning, newspapers had news of a major train accident but in another country.

•   Dog – while dogs are friendly and lovely pets, I have often had dreams in which I have been bitten by a dog on my hands. These have had bad outcomes where my work is con-cerned.

•   Dove – often means the presence of God's Holy Spirit and His favour.

•   Fire – can either mean judgment or a symbol of the Holy Spirit.

•   Fish – catching fish often means success.

- Fruit – ripe fruit often means success. Each time I see visions of ripe fruit, especially when I am expecting some good news at work or some exam results, the outcome has always been good. Sometimes, when faced with decisions regarding the future, visions of fruit have always meant decision leading to prosperity.

If you have been wondering and praying to God, "Is it the right time for me to act now?" The Lord may answer by showing you dreams of ripe fruit. Notice the emphasis I put on prayer because accurate dream interpretation is built on having a relationship with God. That is knowing Him and learning to speak with and listening to His advice and direction.

On the other hand, if you have been living the way of life you really know is against God's teachings in the Bible, this may be a wakeup call before God disciplines you, for He disciplines those He loves. The Bible says it is God who determines the time for everything, time to be born, time to die, time to pray, and time for answered prayers.

"My times are in Your hands…" the Psalmist prayed about his problems to God (Psalm 31:15). And in Ecclesiastes 3: 11, God says He is the One who makes *"everything beautiful and appropriate in its time."*

• Gold – in 2008, I had a dream in which I was carrying three gold bars of different colours, namely, gold, purple, and black. When I mentioned this to my prayer partners, they said that it means I am carrying three special gifts. To be sincere, I was reminded of this dream by the one on germination (below). Up until now, I have always wanted to write a book that would give God glory by sharing my dream experiences with the world but have never been able to do so. Interestingly gold has international value.

• Germination – as I finalised the manuscript of this book, I dreamt three sown seeds bursting out of the ground. I believe these are answers to three main prayers, including publication of this book.

• Halved fruit - On many occasions, I have seen images of halved fruit, and the outcome has been less impressive results. The devourer was at work.

Halved fruit

• Lion – beware of Satan's attacks. Beware also that God may be warning of disobedience. Amos 3 vs 8 says "The lion has roared—so who isn't frightened? The Sovereign Lord has spoken— so who can refuse to proclaim his message?"

• Open doors and windows – in June 2010, I dreamt of coming home to see all the doors to my house open. In the unseen and spiritual realm, this meant my family and loved ones were extremely exposed to attack and that they needed to be secure. The following morning, I prayed to God for protection of every member of my family and relatives. A couple of days later, when I phoned my parents, I was shocked to learn a close relative had been attacked by robbers. Fortunately, he had escaped death—only by a whisker. This confirmed my dream, for only burglars, robbers, and thieves vandalise people's homes and leave doors and windows open as they operate in a hurry and often with violence. Had I not prayed, my relative would have died.

• Problems – Again, as I finalised this book, I had a dream experience where a member of a family I know was in trouble. I asked my wife to agree with me in prayer to cancel Satan's attack on the family. When I phoned another member of that family five minutes later, I was surprised to hear that they had gone to the doctors with a very serious medical problem.

One of the most profound dreams I have ever had was in January 2009. In my dreams, I saw a vision of what seemed to be an airplane in trouble. As an air traveller myself, I was concerned for my own safety, thinking maybe it was a warning about my future travel. I chose not to ignore this vision, as I did not know the meaning. I got out of bed and prayed. To my surprise, the next day, all news channels on TV carried the story of a plane that had a miraculous emergency landing on the Hudson River in USA. All 155 people on board US Airways Flight 1549 from New York's La Guardia airport were saved. In this case, the dream had nothing to do with me, but that God just wanted me to pray. As it turned out, everything that happened was for his glory.

Picture of Hudson River Aircrash

•   Airport - Dreams of going to the airport or at the airport could signify that you are at the gate of acceleration and exponential promotion. Just as we have security, customs and immigration clearances to go through, we need to be ready with our spiritual passports and luggage for a breakthrough.

Have you been experiencing delays in achieving your dreams and aspirations? Have you experienced many disappointments? Pray for God to prepare, accelerate, and bless you in compensation for the time and years lost. *"The LORD says, 'I will give you back what you lost to the swarming locusts, the hopping locusts, the stripping locusts, and the cutting locusts,"* Joel 2 vs 25.

Pray also for your access and entry to be smooth and not to be delayed or denied by the gate keepers. "There is a wide-open door for a great work here, although many oppose me," 1 Corinthians 16 vs 9.

•   Mice, rats, and rodents - pray for protection from things that would destroy the work of your hands.

•   River crossing – you will have a breakthrough or overcome a challenge.

•   Rock – when I was feeling quite vulnerable, I dreamt I was sitting on a rock and surrounded by water. It turned out I was very safe and received all the help I needed.

•   Scoring a goal – winning in a race or scoring a goal whilst playing soccer has always predicted a good outcome.

•   Snake – beware of enemy attack. For example, shortly before I went on a working trip to Mozambique, I dreamt of being bitten by a snake. During the trip, I suffered serious food poisoning and had to spend a night in hospital. Again, fortunately, I had prayed.

•   Strife – any dreams of strife and attack mean spiritual attack. So, pray for protection.

•   Wedding attire— pray for safety. I will explain this in the next chapter.

- Whirlwind and strong winds – pray for protection from spiritual attack.

Finally, just to show how accurate my dreams have been, on one occasion, and I believe these were the early days when God was training me to follow my dreams for their meaning, I dreamt of seeing a needle, and the following morning, I was surprised to see a needle with a thread through its eye on top of the bed I was sleeping on. Until now, my wife and I are not very sure what happened for the needle to be where it was. We only concluded God was good to warn us of its existence.

CHAPTER 8
MISLEADING DREAMS

Not all pictures in a dream show exactly what will happen. The bible says Satan masquerades as an angel of light: 14But I am not surprised! Even Satan disguises himself as an angel of light. So it is no wonder that his servants also disguise themselves as servants of righteousness. In the end, they will get the punishment their wicked deeds deserve. (2 Corinthians 14 – 15)

Through this scripture and some images described in this chapter, God showed me that dream interpretation is a gift of wisdom and discernment only provided by God. Otherwise, if all things manifested as they were seen, then one could argue there is no need to pray after all.

I first became aware of this when I saw a sick person I knew well getting better in a vision, but then in reality, the person died the following morning. Shocked and sad, I asked the Lord why the person died when I had seen him recovering in my dream. The Lord led me to the story of the cup bearer and baker in Genesis 40 vs 8 – 22, whose dreams were interpreted by Joseph. Joseph had asked why his two prison companions looked so sad and miserable that morning.

JOSEPH INTERPRETS TWO DREAMS

Loaves of bread

43

And they replied, "We both had dreams last night, but no one can tell us what they mean."

"Interpreting dreams is God's business," Joseph replied. "Go ahead and tell me your dreams."

So the chief cup-bearer told Joseph his dream first. "In my dream," he said, "I saw a grapevine in front of me. The vine had three branches that began to bud and blossom, and soon it produced clusters of ripe grapes. I was holding Pharaoh's wine cup in my hand, so I took a cluster of grapes and squeezed the juice into the cup. Then I placed the cup in Pharaoh's hand."

"This is what the dream means," Joseph said. "The three branches represent three days. Within three days Pharaoh will lift you up and restore you to your position as his chief cup-bearer. And please remember me and do me a favor when things go well for you. Mention me to Pharaoh, so he might let me out of this place. For I was kidnapped from my homeland, the land of the Hebrews, and now I'm here in prison, but I did nothing to deserve it."

When the chief baker saw that Joseph had given the first dream such a positive interpretation, he said to Joseph, "I had a dream, too. In my dream there were three baskets of white pastries stacked on my head. The top basket contained all kinds of pastries for Pharaoh, but the birds came and ate them from the basket on my head."

"This is what the dream means," Joseph told him. "The three baskets also represent three days. Three days from now Pharaoh will lift you up and impale your body on a pole. Then birds will come and peck away at your flesh."

Pharaoh's birth day came three days later, and he prepared a banquet for all his officials and staff. He summoned his chief cup-bearer and chief baker to join the other officials. He then restored the chief cup-bearer

Interpretation

From this story, one would have thought that, since we all feed on
bread, the dream about bread was good news. But, as it turned out, it was not
so for the baker. A key factor in this dream were the birds, which symbolize
death.

We see this in an amazing story in 1 Samuel 17, where a little boy called
David defeated a Philistine giant by the name Goliath. During the altercation
leading to the battle, David said to Goliath, *"I will kill you and cut off your head…
I will give the dead bodies of your men to the birds and wild animals, and the whole world
will know that there is a God in Israel!"* As it transpired, many Philistines, including
their champion Goliath, died at the hands of David and the Israeli army, and
their bodies were left for birds to eat.

Again, in the book of Judges (Judges 7 vs 8 – 15): is recorded a story of how
God gave Gideon confirmation that he was going to win the battle he and the
people of Israel faced.
Judges 7 vs 8 – 15:

The Midianite camp was in the valley just below Gideon. That night the LORD said, "Get up! Go down into the Midianite camp, for I have given you victory over them! But if you are afraid to attack, go down to the camp with your servant Purah. Listen to what the Midianites are saying, and you will be greatly encouraged. Then you will be eager to attack."

So, Gideon took Purah and went down to the edge of the enemy camp. The armies of Midian, Amalek, and the people of the east had settled in the valley like a swarm of locusts. Their camels were like grains of sand on the seashore—too many to count! Gideon crept up just as a man was telling his companion about a dream. The man said, "I had this dream, and in my dream a loaf of barley bread came tumbling down into the Midianite camp. It hit a tent, turned it over, and knocked it flat!"

His companion answered, "Your dream can mean only one thing—God has given Gideon son of Joash, the Israelite, victory over Midian and all its allies!"

When Gideon heard the dream and its interpretation, he bowed in worship before the LORD. Then he returned to the Israelite camp and shouted, "Get up! For the LORD has given you victory over the Midianite hordes!"

Interpretation

Just as predicted, the Midianites were defeated by Gideon's army of 300 men. To avoid misinterpretation, God Himself interpreted this dream for Gideon through what the two men were saying. Since Gideon was an inexperienced dream interpreter and still learning to hear the voice of God, God wanted to strengthen and assure him of a resounding victory despite his fears that he was clearly outnumbered. Typical of His ways, God was showing Gideon that nothing is impossible with Him – the God who uses *"things the world considers foolish in order to shame those who think they are wise."* (1 Corinthians 1 vs. 27)

PERSONAL EXPERIENCES

I once dreamt of eating bread, and then remembering the bible stories of the baker and Gideon, I chose to pray, protecting my entire family.

That day, when I got back home from work, my wife had a testimony to tell me. She said that she had prepared a delicious casserole dish for dinner. Then shortly before serving it to the children, she discovered that the glass bowl had broken whilst in the oven, leaving bits of glass embedded in the food. She had, therefore, thrown everything in the bin. I could only respond, "Glory to the Most-High God!"

WEDDING APPAREL

Here is another image of deception.

Couple in wedding attire

In my experience, images of weddings have been associated with attack of the family unit or even something worse. I have learnt to pray— saving family and even community members.

Some years ago, I dreamt of seeing a member of church I knew well wearing bridegroom attire. From what the Lord had revealed to me, I took this very seriously and prayed for his protection.

I and the church member attended the same small group. Apparently, in previous small group bible study sessions, I had mentioned that God speaks with people through dreams, but some members in my small group treated this with skepticism.

So, when I had this dream experience, I didn't mention it to my small group members, thinking they would brush me off in the same manner.

However, when the small group met after a fortnight, we were shattered to learn the person I had dreamt of and prayed for was having marriage problems.

We prayed, and fortunately, the marriage was restored a year later. I am fully convinced that the prayer of intercession that I prayed before manifestation of the problem in the natural world played a major part in disrupting Satan's plans in the spirit realm.

Moreover, have you ever noticed that Satan does not like weddings at all? Just consider for a moment how many tragedies you have read in the press or of people you know that struck around wedding times. Just observe and check this out.

My clarion call is to pray for loved ones whenever you have wedding plans in the family and for family protection when you see wedding visions in your dreams.

CHAPTER 9
OTHER DREAMS IN THE BIBLE
AND WHAT GOD CAN DO
FOR YOU

In this chapter, I present all other dreams recorded in the bible, which I had not mentioned in previous chapters.

Creation of woman: After God had created everything else, He created the most beautiful thing on earth: a woman. I am not surprised because God "serves the best wine last." And here is what God has revealed to me, which I think is foundational to understanding why He often talks to us through dreams. In Genesis 2 vs 18 - 23, the bible says:

"Then the LORD God said, 'It is not good for the man to be alone. I will make a helper who is just right for him.' So the LORD God formed from the ground all the wild animals and all the birds of the sky. He brought them to the man to see what he would call them, and the man chose a name for each one. He gave names to all the livestock, all the birds of the sky, and all the wild animals. But still there was no helper just right for him.

So the LORD God caused the man to fall into a deep sleep. While the man slept, the LORD God took out one of the man's ribs and closed up the opening. Then the LORD God made a woman from the rib, and he brought her to the man. 'At last!' the man exclaimed. 'This one is bone from my bone, and flesh from my flesh!'

My interpretation is that the reason why God caused man, to sleep is that, in his natural state and vigour, man is so full of pride with an *"I know everything"* attitude. So, in order to keep man from interfering with His creation of the first woman, Eve, and to keep him from pain, God decided to tranquilise him for a minute whilst He carried out the operation! If He had not done so, I can imagine Adam suggesting to God, "please put this here and that there to make the woman very beautiful."

As you can see, God is God. He does not need man's assistance in doing anything. When He finally presented the woman to the man, Adam could only stand in awe and exclaim, *"At last!"* If we humble ourselves before God, we will see His glory.

Cutting of a covenant: When God wanted to convey the best and important news to Abram (Abraham) that he would have his own son and to show him his future and to do so in a manner that would leave no doubt in Abraham's mind that He would perform what He promised, He sent him to deep sleep and then cut a covenant with him in a dream (Genesis 15).

Decision making: Abimelech, the King of Gerar, was warned by God in a dream not to take Abraham's wife. God can protect you from decisions that can lead to death in a dream (Genesis 20). Friends, pray every day so you can make the right decision in every life circumstance, big or small. They could mean life and death. The "unsinkable" Titanic partly hit an iceberg and sank due to a last-minute decision to drop Second Officer David Blair from the staffing rota in favour of a more experienced Officer. Blair realized much later he had forgotten to hand over keys to the locker where binoculars used for watching out for icebergs were kept.

In the 1912 Presidential race, an obviously Holy Spirit led small decision by US Presidential candidate Teddy Roosevelt to fold his 50 page speech and put it in his breast pocked saved his life when an assailant fired a deadly shot moments before he delivered his public speech.

Business strategy: When Jacob was being cheated in business by his uncle Laban, God intervened by giving Jacob a strategy to prosper and a way out in a dream (Genesis 31 vs 6-13). In this generation where you cannot rely on the world's stock and money market for investment, God can give you one business idea that can change your life through prayer and dreams.

Picture of your future: God often tells people what they will become in future and then works with them to implement the blue-print given. After King David had pleased God by his intentions to build God a temple,

God responded by blessing and showing David how great he was to become. This vision was given to Nathan the prophet during the night and then passed on to King David as a word promise (2 Samuel 7). God can give you a word during your sleep.

One night, I dreamt reading the Book of Psalm 34 vs 29. But when I woke up, I looked up the verse, and to my surprise, there was no such a verse. Psalm 34 ends with verse 22! So rather than being discouraged, I read and received God's word in the entire chapter by faith. Many days later, when I was faced with discouragement, God used Psalm 34 to refresh me.

Wisdom: When King Solomon was faced with the dilemma of being made a king though he was young, inexperienced, and had no clue regarding how to rule a nation, he went to the Source of all wisdom. After worshipping God and giving him the best offering ever given by any king, 1,000 bulls, God appeared to him that very night in a dream and said, "Ask for whatever you want me to give you." Because he had asked for the right thing, God gave King Solomon wisdom, and in addition, wealth and honour (1 Kings 3 vs 4-15). By the way, it was not Solomon's idea to ask for wisdom but his father David's instruction (1 Chronicles 22). So, it's also very important to teach others what the Lord has shown us about His goodness and mercy.

I am convinced that by not paying attention to our dreams, we miss hearing what God yearns to say to us. Provided you keep yourself humble and fear the LORD, your success can mean a lot to your family, future generations, and the kingdom of God. King Solomon's riches were a blessing to the entire nation. *"The king made silver as plentiful in Jerusalem as stone. And valuable cedar timber was as common as the sycamore-fig trees that grow in the foothills of Judah."* (1 Kings 10 vs 27)

God's approval: God appeared again to King Solomon in a dream. This time, it was to show approval of the king's prayers and the temple he had built for God (1 Kings 9 vs 1 – 9).

There are many times I have done some works of righteousness, like giving to the church, helping someone, etc., and God has responded by confirming His approval by showing me showers of blessings in my dreams. This has also happened when I am in need of confirmation of my travel and other plans.

Expression of fear: Our subconscious mind can give us images in dreams, which are clues to our deepest feelings and fears, particularly when our faith and trust in God are going through severe testing. We see this in Job chapter 7 vs 13-14: *"I think, 'My bed will comfort me, and sleep will ease my misery,' but then you shatter me with dreams and terrify me with visions."*
However, the bible clearly shows it is never God's intention to make us afraid. On the contrary, He wants us happy and confident, yet we always put ourselves in a position of fear due to sin and other things that separate ourselves from Him.

Commissioning: Many of the great Old Testament prophets were commissioned by God through visions. Ultimately, their ministry of prophecy was based on this gift of seeing visions.

In a way, I have always believed God commissioned me to my assignment in 1995. When I was born again, God showed me a vision of a huge river with crystal clear water flowing down from the Source I could not see.

Picture of meandering river with crystal clear water

I was on one side of the river, while everything else evil was on the other side. When I woke up, I was filled with unexplainable joy, and deep within me, I knew this was an uncommon and special vision. Since I knew no one who could explain this phenomenon, I was determined to find the meaning from God. I was later led to the word in Revelation 22 vs 1 – 2: *Then the angel showed me a river with the water of life, clear as crystal, flowing from the throne of God and of the Lamb. It flowed down the center of the main street. On each side of the river grew a tree of life, bearing twelve crops of fruit, with a fresh crop each month. The leaves were used for medicine to heal the nations.*

Since I had a passion for giving my tithes to God, I saw my calling vividly from this day onwards. I sensed the LORD was revealing to me that the river stood for the Holy Spirit and His pure word flowing from God's throne. I saw myself as one of the trees planted by the riverside producing good fruit every month (a tithe) and leaves (other good works) to sponsor preaching of the gospel that brings healing and life to the nations. The bible says in Romans 10 vs 14 – 15: *"But how can they call on him to save them unless they believe in him? And how can they believe in him if they have never heard about him? And how can they hear about him unless someone tells them? And how will anyone go and tell them without being sent?..."*

Thus, after this revelation, I felt very confident and bold to serve my LORD with great enthusiasm and no fear. I was commissioned to do what I do for Christ out of gratitude and reverence of Him. The same revelation was confirmed by the word in Ezekiel 47 vs 7 – 12.

Revelation and understanding of who we are: In Daniel chapter 2, God gave king Nebuchadnezzar a dream and vision of what was going to happen to his kingdom and how God's own kingdom was to be established and rule over all kingdoms in the end. He showed the pagan king that all the wealth and everything in his kingdom had actually been given to him by God for His service and purposes.

If you have any questions about your purpose, destiny, and who you are in life, approach God in prayer or by reading or listening to His word, and you will never be disappointed.

Correction: God can use dreams to correct us. This is well illustrated by the second great dream king Nebuchadnezzar was given in Daniel chapter 4. Despite God revealing Himself to the king in the first dream, the king continued to demonstrate pride by thinking he had made himself a powerful king through his own strength and wisdom.

Huge baobab tree that bears fruit

Therefore, God showed him a vision of a huge tree whose top touched the skies and was visible to the ends of the earth. The tree was beautiful and produced abundant food for all. Then a voice from heaven was heard instructing that the tree be cut.

The vision was given to him as a stern warning of imminent judgement and that he should repent in his ways. Unfortunately, the king would not repent, and so judgement fell upon him.

A lesson for all of us is, just as it is important to receive blessings, direction, and guidance from God, it is equally important for people to be aware of and to pay attention when God is warning us when walking in disobedience to His word. But how can we hear warnings and repent in advance of judgment if we haven't trained ourselves to hear God's voice and interpret visions when He is warning us?

Announcement of God's plans: I once read a book which described how a certain Pastor in USA was given a harbinger by God that a hurricane was coming to destroy his town. He was asked to prepare the church and sound alarm bells to his congregation. Unfortunately, some wouldn't listen.

The vision given to the prophet Daniel in Daniel chapter 7 was to warn people of his generation, as well as those to come, about God's end time plan. Again, if we don't stay connected with Him, how are we to receive his predictions and plans?

Guidance: God used dreams to help Joseph make the good decision not to divorce his virgin fiancée Mary when he found out she was carrying baby Jesus through the power of the Holy Spirit (Matthew 1 vs 18 – 25). He also used dreams to guide the three wise men from the east not to return to Herod after seeing baby Jesus and to guide Mary and Joseph to escape to Egypt with baby Jesus and to come back just at the right time (Matthew 2 vs 12 – 23).

In Acts 16 vs 7 – 9, Paul dreamt of seeing a man from Macedonia in Northern Greece *pleading with him, "Come over to Macedonia, and help us!"* Paul and his colleague Silas, therefore, correctly discerned that the Holy Spirit was guiding them to go and preach the gospel in the region of Macedonia instead of Mysia, where they made effort to go yet kept on meeting resistance from the Holy Spirit. Similarly, Cornelius and Peter were given guidance on what to do by God in a vision (Acts 10 vs 1- 20).

By following God's direction, we can be assured to walk in the centre of God's will.

Learn to listen to other people: Through his wife's dreams, Pontius Pilate was warned by God not to pass judgment on Jesus that eventually sent Him to the cross, but he disregarded the wife's message (Matthew 27 vs 19).

I have taught my wife to always pay attention to her dreams. The reward has been we have effectively prayed for and averted many potential family disasters.

Being used as God's vessel: We can train ourselves to be ready to be used as God's special vessels by learning to hear from Him through dreams and visions, amongst many other communication channels. In Acts 9 vs 10 – 19, Ananias was approached by God in a vision to go and pray for Paul and to commission him for God's work. Paul, previously known as Saul, was struck blind by a light from the LORD Jesus Christ whilst on a mission to Damascus to kill Christians. His vision was only restored three days later after Ananias had prayed for him. Paul was used mightily by Jehovah to preach the gospel of Good News mostly to non-Jewish non-believers in modern day Europe. He is the author of the majority of the Books in the New Testament!

CHAPTER 10
HERE IS HOW IT WORKS

If you want to appropriate the things of God, you have to do it by faith. Be intentional about learning how to apply the newly revealed word of God to you in everyday life. Start by believing that the man or woman sent with revelation of God's word is indeed a messenger from God.

I will give you an everyday example that will help you understand what I mean.

On a bright summer day, I heard man of God, Dr. Jerry Savelle, preaching about the Favour and Blessing of God. I liked the message he was teaching so much, and wanted to appropriate it by faith for my benefit.

He read from Genesis 12 vs 2 – 3 of The Amplified Bible translation, which reads:

"And I will make of you a great nation, and I will bless you [with abundant increase of favors] and make your name famous and distinguished, and you will be a blessing [dispensing good to others].

And I will bless those who bless you [who confer prosperity or happiness upon you] and curse him who curses or uses insolent language toward you; in you will all the families and kindred of the earth be blessed [and by you they will bless themselves]."

Dr. Savelle explained that the blessing of the LORD is an empowerment to prosper and overcome in every situation and that the favour of the LORD opens doors of opportunity and causes people to do good things for you they would not normally do for anybody else. He said if you have accepted Jesus Christ as your LORD and Saviour, the blessing and favour of God was automatically given to you. He gave an example of Abraham, who believed God's promise above, and when you look at his life in Genesis 13 to 25, you find that he became rich even in famine. And, when his nephew Lot was abducted, Abraham mobilised 300 servants from his household and tracked down the enemy forces, recovering everything they had looted, including Lot.

This happened because of the blessing and abundant favour of God upon Abraham.

As time went on, Abraham and Sarah, at 100 and 90 years old respectively, overcame barrenness. They died many years later, having enjoyed long life, and nowhere in the bible do we read that they were ever sick. Their descendants were equally blessed.

When I heard this powerful message, I prayed, *"LORD, thank You for the word and promise You have given me. I receive it and declare that I am blessed and highly favoured like Abraham was. Now LORD, teach me how to apply this knowledge and see Your blessing and favour manifest in my life every day, beginning right now!"*

My daughter asked me to do her a favour. *"Daddy, if you get a moment, could you please post this parcel for me? The deadline is today, and this really has to go!"*

I prayed again, *"LORD, as I go to the Post Office, teach me and show me what the favour and blessing of God looks like in practise."*

After walking for ten minutes, I reached my local Post Office. Then, I nearly passed out when I saw a sign at the Post Office counter in the off-license shop that operates the Post Office. It read, "Closed! Will open again at 6am tomorrow morning. Sorry for the inconvenience!"

A shop assistant, who was busy packing groceries in the isles, approached me with an apology and explanation of why the postal service, which was normally available from 6am to 10pm, was closed at 4:30 pm that day. She then directed me to the nearest other Post Office, a mile away.

Instead of complaining and despising the outcome of my prayer relating to the word I had heard from Dr. Savelle, I said, *"Thank You, LORD, that I am blessed and highly favoured! I know Your word is the truth, and I believe the reason why the Post Office is closed today is that Satan is trying to discourage me so he can steal God's word just sown in my heart. He is rattled and scared that if I catch understanding of how the blessing and favour of God works, I will share it and bless all people around the world! Thank You for the opportunity You have just given me to walk another mile. It's a blessing because I am going to exercise my body and have good health. Furthermore, I am going to enjoy another hour of this gorgeous summer weather. Thank You, Jesus, for the truth that the steps of a righteous man are ordered of the LORD."*

As I walked to my next destination, I met some strangers walking their dog, and they greeted me. I took the time to thank the LORD for the blessing and favour of being greeted by strangers! I said to myself that if I wasn't blessed and highly favoured, these people might not have greeted but cursed me in their hearts. Some twenty minutes later, whilst sauntering on the pedestrian walkway, a cyclist shot past me from behind.

Again, I took a moment to thank the LORD for His favour that protects me like a "shield" (Psalm 5:12). The reason? I could have been accidentally hit by the cyclist because I wasn't seeing him approach me. Several minutes later, I saw new houses, a church, and other things I had never seen before despite driving along the same route many times. When I reached the next Post Office, they were four minutes away from closing for the day, and so, they accepted my parcel, remarking, *"Sorry, we can't send it today but first thing in the morning. Hope that's alright with you!"*

Then the LORD made me aware of the meaning of the blessing of the LORD. I suddenly realised that I had overcome the challenge of failing to meet my daughter's objective to send the parcel that day. Though it could not be transported physically on that day, at least there was now a receipt, i.e. evidence of dispatch of the parcel by the stipulated deadline!

On the way back home, I walked past a block of flats where I overheard a couple quarrelling and shouting at each other with children crying. The LORD prompted me to pray for the deliverance of the couple from strife. He said to me, *"Son, I have given you My blessing so that you can be a solution wherever I send you."* I prayed to the LORD, quoting Ezekiel 22 vs 30, which says, *"I searched for someone to stand in the gap in the wall so I wouldn't have to destroy the land, but I found no one."* I said to the LORD, "Here I am praying and fulfilling Your word which says you shall be a blessing to all families in the earth!"

Although I will never know the outcome of my prayer, at least this side of Heaven (on earth), I believe that God blessed that family with the peace they needed so much because a blessed man loved and cared to pray for them!

As you can see, by becoming intentional to pray to the LORD, asking how I could apply the revelation given to me on the blessing and favour of

God, the LORD taught me how to appropriate it through a seemingly insignificant walk to the Post Office.

So dear reader, I implore you to receive by faith the revelation I am giving you, that one of the many ways God speaks with people is through dreams. Before going to bed each time, pray and ask the LORD to reveal to you through dreams the good plans He has in store for you and the bad things the devil is planning to destroy your life. Ask Him to help you remember the dreams and teach you how to interpret them. Ask Him to bless and protect you as He reveals how the dreams really manifest in life.

As in the above example, you may initially struggle and get disappointed with the seemingly negative results. But if you talk with other believers, read Christian books and the bible, watch Christian TV, (my favourite channels are God TV, TBN and Daystar TV) or observe the small and big things happening in your life after bad or good dreams, you will be amazed at the clues you see that relate to the dreams you saw.

Once you begin to see some links, always thank the LORD, knowing that He will increase your understanding if you show appreciation for the little things He shows you initially. *"I will honor those who honor me, and I will despise those who think lightly of me,"* says the LORD in 1 Samuel 2 vs 20.

I will end with a couple of bad dreams, and how in every dream, good or bad, God always shows you His favour and blessing.

During a season of difficulty, I had a weird nightmare in which I found myself clinging for dear life at the apex of a very tall cylindrical tower! Never mind how I had gotten up there in the first place, I was trying in desperation to slide down but couldn't do it because of the sheer height. I suddenly woke up from this horrible dream, obviously scared.

After a prayer of asking God to cancel whatever this dream meant and for it to never happen to me and my family, I found myself being drawn to the scripture which reads: *1 When the Lord brought back his exiles to Jerusalem, it was like a dream! We were filled with laughter, and we sang for joy. And the other nations said, "What amazing things the Lord has done for them." Yes, the Lord has done amazing things for us! What joy! Restore our fortunes, Lord, as streams renew the desert.* (Psalm 126 vs 1 – 4)

Instead of being gripped with fear, I believed God's word above. I took it by faith that since I was in an impossible situation in real life, the LORD was going to suddenly and miraculously deliver me in the same manner that I woke up from that horrible dream— only to realise it was merely a dream. Just like the children of Israel were delivered from their impossible captivity and it seemed so unreal, the LORD was going to supernaturally deliver me liked He did for the children of Israel.

In another dream the other night, I dreamed of seeing a rat in our kitchen. I tried to kill it in my dream but in vain. Though we have never seen such pests anywhere in our houses in this part of the world, I knew God was warning me of a spiritual pest that wanted to eat, gnaw, destroy, and mess up my life. I cooperated with the LORD and prayed for protection and that he would show me His blood redemption from all bad things. Then, the Holy Spirit reminded me of a scripture about rats!

1 Samuel chapters 4, 5, and 6 tell the story of the battle between the children of Israel and the Philistines. Israel was defeated, and in the next battle, they thought they would win if they brought God's Ark of the Covenant to the battlefield. To their utter surprise, the unthinkable happened. Israel was defeated, and the Ark of the LORD was captured! Israel fled whilst the Philistines took the Ark of God and put it in their temple in front of the statue of Dagon, their god. But to their surprise, each morning, they found Dagon knocked down and lying on the floor. The LORD also *"caused [mice to spring up and there was] very deadly destruction and He smote the people with [very painful] tumors or boils."*

This happened from city to city, wherever the Philistines tried to take the Ark of the Covenant of God. After seven months of destruction, the Philistine priests and elders came to their senses and decided to return the Ark of the Covenant back to Israel along with gift offerings of gold moulded in the shape of the deadly mice and tumors. With this, the destruction ended.

Again, given the context of my dream – an impossible situation in real life, I took by faith the above bible message to mean what was meant for evil and seemed tricky for me to solve (represented by the elusive rat), the Lord was well able to overcome by reversing the situation. Friends, just like the Ark of the Covenant was returned to its rightful owners, God will always make sure what belongs to you will be returned back to you, with interest.

You will already have seen by now that real interpretation of dreams originates from knowing what is written in the bible, i.e., God's word. Many committed Christians read the entire bible many times during their life time. Their knowledge is like that of a diligent librarian who knows where to find every book and author in stock in their library.

I don't want to mislead you to think that I have read the entire bible a couple or many times, but I can assure you that I will never regret the one time I read through it. I challenge you to do it so you can benefit from a good helicopter view of how God thinks, speaks, and relates to all people He has created. Hosea 4 vs 6, *"My people are being destroyed because they don't know me."*

CHAPTER 11
THE LORD IS MY SHEPHERD

I am forever grateful to Father God for giving us the LORD Jesus Christ as our perfect model for life. Since Jesus is the Son of Almighty God and the only person that ever-lived life here on earth without sinning, we are tempted to think that He never experienced any trouble. Yet, His entire life was marked with trouble and sorrows right from the beginning to the end. When the time of His birth came, there was no decent place for Him to be born, except a stable or low-class lodging His earthly parents rented in Bethlehem because *"there was no place for them in the inn"* (Luke 2:7).

His humble first bed was a manger – a feeding box for cattle, horses, sheep, etc., and some poor shepherds were His first visitors. When word of His arrival spread around, king Herod felt threatened at the birth of a new King and *"gave orders to kill all the boys in Bethlehem and its vicinity who were two years old"* (Matthew 2:16). Through a dream given to Joseph by an Angel, Joseph and Mary, along with baby Jesus, were able to escape to Egypt, where they stayed for a while.

The entire bible— in particular, the four gospels of Matthew, Mark, Luke, and John— show us that a major part of Jesus' ministry was replete with suffering from threats, opposition, and ill-treatment by the Sadducees, Pharisees, and the Jewish leaders of His day. They eventually influenced the people of Israel and the Roman authorities to crucify Him, with His last words of suffering and pain, *"My God, my God, why have You forsaken me?"* (Matthew 27:46)

If the Son of God could not be spared from suffering, what more you and me? I can testify to that.

There are many times in my life that I have felt like God has forsaken me with no clear answers to prayer or guidance through dreams! But God has always been faithful in encouraging and showing me the comfort of His love through inspiration from His word in the bible.

For example, I am inspired to know that during his life and ascension to power, David suffered great persecution from his predecessor king, Saul, who wanted to kill him out of envy and jealousy because David was more popular than him after killing Goliath, the feared Philistine giant.

He experienced the pain of having a daughter raped by her own half-brother, death of three children as a result of subterfuge, revenge, and undermining of his kingdom by ambitious sons, Absalom and Adonijah. David also fought countless wars with the Philistines and other nations surrounding Israel, yet he was the chosen and beloved of God. He is the one who also penned the famous Psalm 23, which reads:

1 The Lord is my shepherd, I lack nothing. He makes me lie down in green pastures, he leads me beside quiet waters, he refreshes my soul. He guides me along the right paths for his name's sake. Even though I walk through the darkest valley, I will fear no evil, for you are with me; your rod and your staff, they comfort me. You prepare a table before me in the presence of my enemies. You anoint my head with oil; my cup overflows. Surely your goodness and love will follow me all the days of my life, and I will dwell in the house of the Lord forever.

The long and short message of David in this Psalm is that we are made for God and that He cares for us so much that we do not lack any good thing.

I have now discovered that when God seems distant, and not answering my prayers or showing me direction through dreams, He is busy shaping my heart. I have learned to submit my life to Jesus my Lord, and to give Him His right to be my Shepherd as written in Psalm 23.

Friends, when experiencing bad seasons in our lives, let us be aware that Satan, the Devil, the Serpent cannot do anything unless he first gets permission from our Heavenly Father. The word of God reveals and explains all the hidden and difficult things we go through in life but, do not understand. We see this in the troubles Job went through, and that these were caused by Satan, (Job chapters 1 and 2). God allows storms in our lives to shake up the confidence we tend to have in ourselves and to show us we need Him and that He is always with us, both in good and the bad times we find ourselves walking through the valleys with shadows of death. Here is how we know. When experiencing financial trouble, just ask yourself this question: Who has been paying my bills and who has been providing my food? Likewise, if you are sick, ask yourself: Who has been taking care of me, and do I deserve the love being shown to me by all people caring for me? The deeper truth and answer to these questions is that, behind it all, is the LORD, our Shepherd. *"The Lord directs the steps of the godly. He delights in every detail of their lives. Though they stumble, they will never fall, for the Lord holds them by the hand."* (Psalm 37 vs 23 – 24.)

If you are suffering, know that the LORD, who is in full control, sometimes allows us to go through stuff so that when we make it, we will be a source of encouragement to others. *"He comforts us in all our troubles so that we can comfort others. When they are troubled, we will be able to give them the same comfort God has given us."* (2 Corinthians 1 vs 4)

As I have already mentioned, dreams filtered through the word of God for meaning play a big role in my life, and I hope this book will also help you discover how God has been desiring all along to speak with you and show you His love in the tranquil state of sleep. Although God speaks to us through dreams, He has many other ways of communicating with us. He can also speak through our conscience and inner conviction of heart – that unexplained knowing of what is right or wrong, particularly where the bible is not specific about what to do.

He speaks through the written word of God in the bible, which is His revealed will. He can speak through a prophetic word. For example, someone can say something that confirms a course of action you may have been praying to God about, and believing that He wanted you take, yet you were not very sure it was Him speaking to you. Naturally, that person would not be in a position to know that you were having issues related to what they would have said. God also speaks through the counsel of Godly men and women He has put in your life — please listen to them as this is very important. Additionally, God speaks through provision for what He may be calling you to do. Remember the story of Elijah in 1 Kings Chapter 17? God instructed Elijah to go and hide in the Kerith Ravine, where he was to drink water from the brook and be supernaturally fed by some ravens sent by God. When the brook dried, God sent him to Zarephath in the region of Sidon, where he was to be fed by a poor widow.

As well as this, Colossians 3:15 also encourages us to let the peace of mind be the umpire whenever we are making important decisions. The LORD has manifold ways of communicating with His children, including through nature and circumstances. For example, when doors continue to be shut, this may mean God has something in store for you, greater than what you are aiming at.

Sometimes, I have prayed, "LORD give me a sign that this is what you are saying to me," and He often shows me the covenant sign of a rainbow.

Where does this come from? We learn this from how the LORD led the children of Israel through the desert. Can you imagine God leading them by a cloud? Whenever the cloud moved, they moved, and whenever it stopped, they set up camp. That means, other people who were seeing the same cloud thought it was just another ordinary cloud, yet to the children of Israel, this was a sign from God to either advance or set up camp. All these ways are inspired by the Holy Spirit, who gives man gifts, revelation, and understanding of the ways of God. In other words, in our generation, it is the Holy Spirit who guides and leads us. John 16 verse 13 in the Bible says, *"But when He, the Spirit of truth comes, He will guide you into all truth …,"* and the way He does it is, He will give you thoughts, promptings, ideas, signs, dreams, and visions, etc., that will always align with the written word of God in situations where your own human wisdom, feelings, and understanding would lead you otherwise.

My experience is that, since we access the things of God by faith and faith itself involves taking risks, we need to employ an odd number of at least three ways above to confirm His direction, the primary of which is listening to the Holy Spirit and God's written word.

Here is also one good observation I have made with dreams. Much depends on the context, that is, what is really happening in my life. When I am going through dark seasons in life and then dream dark dreams in which I escape from trouble miraculously, I pray, thanking God for giving me encouragement that the outcome will be good. I will still continue to pray hard for my deliverance, including doing everything I know and must do in the natural to protect myself or succeed in the situation. When facing a major decision in life, I have now learnt never to turn right or left, proceed or retreat without the Holy Spirit confirming that, not just by dreams, but in several other forms.

Again, knowing who the Holy Spirit is, His works, and how to fellowship with Him amongst the trinity is the principal thing. The good thing is we can start from wherever we are by praying to God, asking for forgiveness of our sins, and inviting Him into our lives. We can then ask that He reveals Himself to us in a way we will recognize Him for ourselves as God the Father, the Son (Jesus Christ), and the Holy Spirit.

Finally, I have learned that when God gives you a dream about something good or bad going to happen, understand that this may not happen immediately and automatically.

Take the dream of Joseph in Genesis 37 verses 5 – 9, and here is a young man given a vision that he was going to become "Prime Minister" of Egypt. But the next series of events— being sold by his brothers to some Ishmaelite traders who took him to Egypt, working as Potiphar's slave in Egypt, being falsely accused of attempting to rape his master's wife, and ending up in jail— did not look like the dream God gave him was going to be fulfilled.

It's after many years of suffering injustice that Joseph was finally called out of prison and made "Prime Minister" after wisely interpreting a dream that God had given Pharaoh, predicting a seven-year period of great agricultural success followed by a seven-year period of famine. When given a dream and we recognize the good thing God is trying to communicate to us, we need to pray and continue believing that God will do what He promised despite circumstances.

Interestingly, after Joseph was shown the two dreams about his future, we do not read anywhere else that he ever dreamt again. I can imagine him asking God to show him through dreams when his slavery to Potiphar was going to end and how he was actually going to come out of jail. But, none of those details were revealed to him. Instead, the bible shows us that Joseph's own sudden deliverance from prison came when he started using the gift of dream interpretation to help others!

The message is this: the gift of dream interpretation and every other gift, skill, or ability the Lord gives you is meant to be a blessing to you and others. It's for the glory and purposes of God, and we have to always reciprocate His kindness for blessing and delivering us from all our troubles by being thankful. This is the reason why I am sharing with the world what God has taught me through dreams.

> "Give thanks to the Lord and call out to him! Tell
> the nations what he has done! Sing to him; sing
> praises to him. Tell about the amazing things he has
> done." (1 Chronicles 16: 8 – 9)

CHAPTER 12
CONCLUSION

As you can see, I have touched only the tip of an iceberg, because no man could possibly know, let alone understand all the visions a man can be given by God in a dream.

I am an ordinary person and not a superman. In James chapter 5 vs 17 - 18, the bible says, *Elijah was as human as we are, and yet when he prayed earnestly that no rain would fall, none fell for three and a half years! Then, when he prayed again, the sky sent down rain and the earth began to yield its crops.*

The only *"qualification"* I have for me to know the meaning of my own dreams is that I have learned to humble myself and ask Someone who knows all things.

Many people miss the road or spend money on things they didn't really like to buy mainly because they just did not bother to ask, and if they did ask, maybe they asked the wrong person.

Dreams are given to everybody, but interpretation of their meaning is a special gift from God. If you don't "dream," maybe it's just that you don't pay attention. All I have managed to do in this book is to lay the biblical foundation and principles that could help you understand the meaning of your own dreams. The main one is to ask God for the meaning of your dreams.

1 Corinthians 2 vs 10 – 14 perfectly sums up everything:

But it was to us that God revealed these things by his Spirit. For his Spirit searches out everything and shows us God's deep secrets. No one can know a person's thoughts except that person's own spirit, and no one can know God's thoughts except God's own Spirit. And we have received God's Spirit (not the world's spirit), so we can know the wonderful things God has freely given us.

When we tell you these things, we do not use words that come from human wisdom. Instead, we speak words given to us by the Spirit, using the Spirit's words to explain spiritual truths. But people who aren't spiritual can't receive these truths from God's Spirit. It all sounds foolish to them and they can't understand it, for only those who are spiritual can understand what the Spirit means.

I hope I have inspired you to seek true wisdom from God, the real Source of all wisdom and Creator of the Universe.

If you do not know Him, I recommend you pray this simple prayer to receive the LORD Jesus Christ, for God's word says, "Jesus told him, and 'I am the way, the truth, and the life. No one can come to the Father except through me." (John 14 vs 6)

LORD Jesus, I am a sinner. Please forgive all my sins. I want to know You more and to receive You as my LORD and Saviour. I believe You died for me and paid the full price for all my sins, iniquities, and transgressions on the cross. You rose from the dead and ascended into heaven and are sitting by the right hand of God the Father, where You rule the entire Universe. Give me the gift of Your Holy Spirit and all the gifts of the Spirit, including the one on dreams and visions and their interpretation.

I believe that, by this prayer, I am now a born-again child of the Most-High God and now have a new beginning.

In Jesus' Name I pray. Amen!

If you have done this, go to the church nearest to where you live every Sunday for more teachings on who God is and to grow the relationship He has with you.

Ask also for information on the ALPHA course (www.alpha.org)

For further study on the meaning and interpretation of dreams, the Lord recently (2019) blessed me with a fantastic book I read, entitled "the Dream Book – A beginner's guide to understanding God's voice while you sleep" written by Stephanie Schureman. I strongly recommend it.

I also recommend you read Pastor Rick Warren's book entitled "The Purpose Driven Life – What on earth am I here for?" This will help you understand why God created you including His mission and assignment for you.